"Come and See KIDS"

Catholic Bible Study
for Children

In the Beginning

by
Laurie Watson Manhardt, PhD

Illustrated by
Aileen Co
and
Melissa Dayton

Crafts by
Sandra Beyer

EMMAUS
ROAD
PUBLISHING

Steubenville, Ohio
A Division of Catholics for the Faith

Emmaus Road Publishing
827 North Fourth Street
Steubenville, Ohio 43952

Library of Congress Control Number 2006937128
ISBN: 978-1-931018-42-5

Nihil obstat: Monsignor Joseph N. Rosie, *Censor Librorum*
Imprimatur: @ John M. Smith
Bishop of Trenton
June 15, 2003

The *nihil obstat* and *imprimatur* are official declarations
that a book is free of doctrinal or moral error.

Cover design and layout by
Jacinta Calcut
Image Graphics & Design
Ann Arbor, Michigan

Cover artwork:
The Separation of Land and Water, Michelangelo Buonarroti

Melissa Dayton's artwork can be found at
www.pearlsofgracefineart.com

For additional information on the
"Come and See - Catholic Bible Study" series visit
www.CatholicBibleStudy.net

In the Beginning

Introduction

"In The Beginning" provides an opportunity for young children to study the Bible while their mothers are doing Bible study. **"In The Beginning"** tells stories from the book of Genesis in language that a pre-school or early elementary school child can understand. Each story is followed by an illustration that the child can color and a craft for the child to make.

The twofold benefit of blessing the children, while at the same time serving the mother with an opportunity to share her home study lesson in a small group without distraction, can be achieved when there are volunteers who feel called by God to serve as children's teachers.

Nurslings and small infants may stay in the small group with their mothers without distracting the other women in the group. Toddlers are best served by babysitters. Concern should be taken that a baby-sitter is minding an appropriate number of children to afford safety and a peaceful environment. If sufficient babysitters are not available, women can take turns volunteering to mind the children. Each woman will want to serve by helping with the children, whether she has children of her own in the program, or not. High school students and grandmothers also make wonderful babysitters and children's teachers.

Children's teachers must have a love for God and a love for children. Formal education or teaching experience is not necessary. However, children's teachers and babysitters must meet the requirements of the parish and diocese for working with children.

Children from the ages of approximately two to five years of age could be served in a classroom setting, depending on their readiness and comfort in separating from their mothers. The children's teacher will be flexible in allowing the mother to stay with the child for awhile and expect the child to cry a bit for the first few times when Mom leaves.
Initially, children could be allowed some playtime with toys, books, or blocks. After playtime, when all of the children have arrived, the children's teacher will make the Sign of the Cross, say a short prayer, and read the Bible story for the day to the children. The children can then color the accompanying picture, and work on crafts. Older children can work with pasting or cutting out figures. Children and teachers can act out the Bible story. Sing songs, march around the room, and have fun. Try to sing and repeat the memory verse with the children.

A simple snack of animal crackers and water or goldfish crackers and juice could be offered. Mothers might take turns bringing snacks or contribute money to purchase snacks. Remember to avoid nuts and chocolate, as some children may have allergies.

Small children memorize Bible verses well, often better than adults. Repetition helps the child remember the verse and the concept. Putting the verse to music can be a big help in learning Scripture. Try to fit the verse to a simple children's melody such as "Three Blind Mice" or "Frère Jacque." Singing makes memorizing easier for children. Memory verses can be repeated often during the day and again from week to week.

Each chapter of **"Come and See KIDS: In The Beginning"** includes a:
- **Bible Story** from "The Book of Genesis," followed by a
- **Picture** describing that story, which the child can color, and a
- **Children's Craft,** illustrated and explained in detail.

The children's teacher should read over the craft in advance, obtain necessary supplies, and make a sample of the craft to show the children. After the teacher tells the Bible story, the children may act out the story and then make the craft.

Children can prepare a simple program of recitation, singing, or drama to share with the adults at Christmastime or at the end of the class year. Everyone enjoys seeing the children perform, even if the children's teacher is doing most of the singing or reciting. It is wonderful to see the children God has given us singing about Him.

A small group of children may be taught in one room. A larger number of children can be divided into age groups with small children in one room and older children in another. A cooperative program in which mothers take turns teaching the children could also be considered.

Pray about what will work best in your situation. Support a culture of life. Try to welcome and embrace all of the mothers and children God sends your way. Please make sure that children's teachers also have an opportunity to share their home study questions in a group later. The teacher could offer to stay after Bible study with the children's teachers and show them a video-tape of the adult lesson.

Essentially, pray for the children. Love the children. Be patient. Serve the mothers and children for the glory of God. Do the best you can with the resources you have. God doesn't expect perfection. He simply invites you to do your best for Him.

Pray, serve, and give God the glory!

In the Beginning Was God

Genesis 1

Memory Verse:
"In the beginning God made heaven and earth."
(Genesis 1:1)

How old are you? Do you know how old Mommy and Daddy are? Grandma and Grandpa might be sixty or seventy or even eighty years old. How old you are shows how long you have lived on this earth. God knew you even before you were born, when Mommy carried you under her heart.

Do you know how old God is? God is eternal. God doesn't have a birthday, because God always was and always will be, forever and ever, until the end of time, millions and billions and trillions of years from now.

God the Father, Jesus Christ, and the Holy Spirit have existed for all time, without a beginning or an end. This is a mystery. It is too amazing for our minds to understand. Yet, we believe this is true, even though our minds can't take it all in. We accept on faith that God is everlasting. God gave you the gift of faith, so that you can believe in Him and trust in Him, even when you can't understand.

The very first words of the Bible are "In the beginning was God." God was already there at the beginning of time. Human beings, like you and me, are born, live our lives, and then die. When we die, we hope to go to heaven, see Jesus face-to-face, and live with God forever.

God is not bound by space or time. God can be everywhere at the same time. He can be up in heaven and here on earth. God can be in the jungles of Africa, and on the beach in Florida, and on an iceberg in Alaska, all at the same time. Isn't God amazing?

Don't ever be afraid, because God is always with you. God always watches over you. God loves you with an everlasting love. God has always loved you, and always will love you. God will never leave you. God is always near.

Glory be to the Father,
and to the Son, and to the Holy Spirit,
as it was in the beginning,
is now, and ever shall be,
world without end.
Amen.

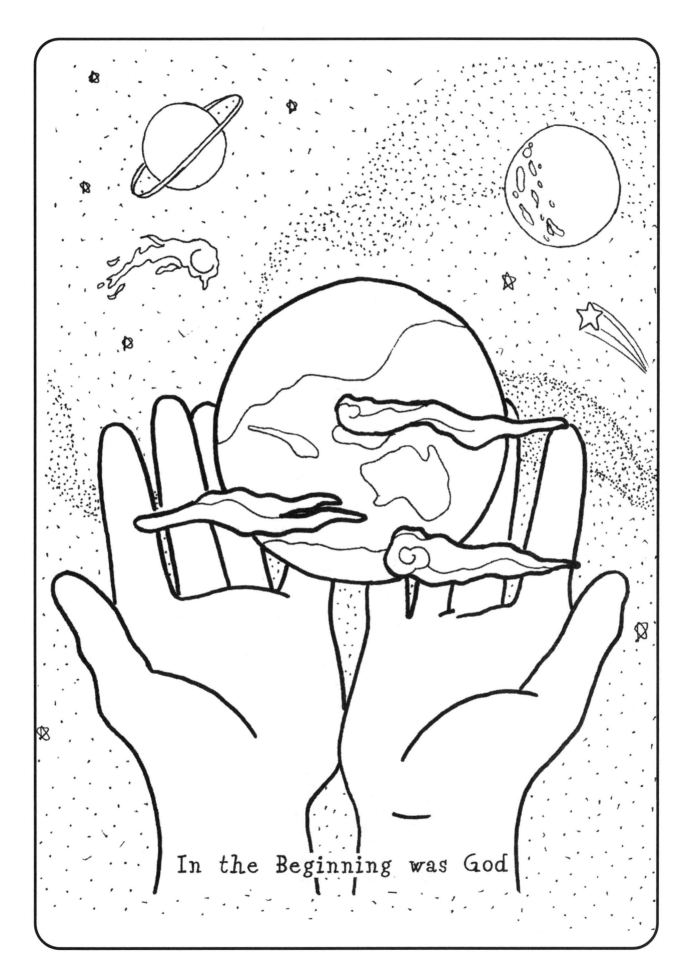

In the Beginning was God

The children will make a self-portrait craft that will remind them of God's everlasting love for them.

Materials:
White paper, colored construction paper, crayons, glue sticks, markers, and scissors.

Preparation:
1. Trace and cut a circle (about the size of a large drinking glass or mug) to use as a pattern.
2. Fold and cut colored construction paper in half (short sides together).

Assembling:
1. Trace the circle pattern on white construction paper. Cut it out.
2. Glue the circle in the middle of the colored construction paper.
3. Draw a self-portrait using the circle as the child's head (have them draw their eyes, nose, and mouth first and then add hair and finishing touches).
4. Write "God Loves" in large letters above the picture and then the child's name below their portrait.

Other ideas:
1. Add a frame around the completed craft using craft sticks or construction paper.
2. For younger children, pre-cut the white circles.
3. For older children, use colored yarn as hair in their portrait.

THE SIGN OF THE CROSS

In the name of the Father,

and of the Son,

and of the Holy Spirit.

Amen.

Creation

Genesis 1:1-25

Memory Verse:
"God made everything and it was good."
(Genesis 1:21)

God said, "Let there be light;" and there was light (Genesis 1:3). God created the sun, moon, and stars, and there was evening and morning, night and day. On the second day, God said, "Let's separate heaven from the waters below" (Genesis 1:6). When God said this, it happened just as He said. On the third day, God said, "Let's gather the waters together in one place and let the dry land appear" (Genesis 1:9). And so there were oceans and lakes and rivers, with dry land all around them. God called the dry land earth and the waters He called seas. "And God saw that it was good" (Genesis 1:10).

Then God made plants and trees. So there were grapes, nuts, olives, dates, and figs to eat. Then, God made birds to fly in the sky and fish to swim in the sea. God made animals of every kind: dogs and cats, pigs and cows, horses, zebras, lions, tigers, and bears.

Oh, my! Some of the animals could be pets, like kittens and puppies. Other animals would produce good food. Cows give us milk. Chickens lay eggs. God made everything for us to enjoy, and everything that God made was good. God is a good God, all the time. And everything He does for us, He does in love.

God made everything out of nothing. God speaks, and whatever God says happens. All creation obeys the voice of God, and we should obey too.

Mommy can make a cake if she has flour and sugar and eggs, but she can't make a cake out of nothing. Daddy could make you a playhouse if he had some lumber and a hammer and nails. But Daddy couldn't make it if he didn't have any wood. You can make a pretty picture for Grandma if you have paper and some crayons. But God can make something out of nothing. Indeed, God made everything out of nothing. Isn't God amazing? Isn't God good? What do you think is the very best thing that God created? God created you!

The children will make a "creation vase" while examining the wonderful objects God created.

Materials:
Small empty tissue boxes, light blue and yellow felt, nature objects and dried wildflowers, glue, and scissors.

Preparation:
1. Collect various kinds of nature objects and dried wildflowers that can be placed into the vase. Some examples are sticks with attached leaves or acorns, pine branches with small pine cones, pleasant smelling dried herbs, and other various dried flowers.

2. Cut medium-sized circles and small triangles of yellow felt (to create a sun).

Assembling:
1. Create the vase by gluing the light blue felt around the outside of the tissue box, leaving the top alone.

2. Glue the yellow circle on the tissue box and then add the small triangles around the circle to create a sun.

3. Place God's created objects into the vase. Be careful not to overload the vase because it may tip over (each object should stick out about 4"-5"). Cut the objects to fit.

Other ideas:
1. Glue small "creation" objects outside the tissue box (acorns, leaves, flowers, pictures of birds, butterflies, etc.).

2. For younger children, pre-cut smaller pieces of felt to cover the tissue box rather than wrapping the felt around the box.

3. Older children can cut and glue the felt to the entire vase.

4. Add a small piece of foam to the inside of the vase and secure each nature object into it.

Adam and Eve

Genesis 1:26–2:25

Memory Verse:
"God made man in His image."
(Genesis 1:26)

God said, "Let's make man in our image and likeness" (Genesis 1:26). And so, God created man in the image and likeness of God. God saved the best for last. God made man with a brain to understand the difference between good and evil. Man knows right from wrong. God created man with a soul that will live forever. God named the first man Adam.

Adam was lonely. He didn't have anyone to play with, or talk to, or do things with. Have you ever felt lonely and needed to be with someone? God knew that Adam was lonely, and God said, "It isn't good for man to be all alone" (Genesis 2:18). So, God put Adam to sleep, took a rib from Adam's side, and made a woman, named Eve, to be his helpmate. When Adam woke up, he was very happy to see Eve. Adam said, "This at last is bone of my bone and flesh of my flesh" (Genesis 2:23).

God told Adam and Eve to be fruitful and multiply. God gave them everything they needed to be happy. Adam and Eve lived in the Garden of Eden. The garden was very beautiful, and they found delicious food to eat. Adam and Eve were very happy in the Garden of Eden. They walked in the garden and talked to each other and they talked to God.

Adam named all the animals in the garden. If Adam said, "dog," then that was its name. If Adam said, "hippopotamus" or "zebra," then that was its name. God let Adam name all of the animals. How many animals can you name?

Adam and Eve were the first man and woman on earth. They married each other in the sight of God and started the first family. Did you know that Adam and Eve were the very first husband and wife? Adam was the first father, and Eve was the first mother. The very first wedding took place in the Garden of Eden. Have you ever been to a wedding? What special clothes did the bride and groom wear? Did you know that you were created in the image and likeness of God?

Adam and Eve

This special craft will make an individualized "thumbprint bookmark" showing how unique and loved each child is to God.

Materials:
Foam paper, colorful ribbon, ink pad, wipes, thin markers, curvy scissors, and hole puncher.

Preparation:
1. Create a bookmark from the foam paper. First, trace lines on the foam paper to make 4"x2" rectangles. Then cut the bookmarks out using the curvy scissors.
2. Cut strips of ribbon about 6" long (one per craft).
3. Punch a hole in the center of one of the bookmark's shorter ends.

Assembling:
1. Take each child's thumb and carefully press it in the ink pad and then onto the center of the bookmark creating the thumbprint.
2. Use wipes to clean their fingers.
3. Write the child's name under the thumbprint using markers (if possible, let the child do this).
4. Draw a happy face using the thin black marker on the thumbprint (don't forget to add eyelashes for girls).
5. Write "I'm Thumb-body Special" above the child's thumbprint.
6. Thread the ribbon through the hole and tie a knot and bow.

Other ideas:
1. Decorate the bookmark with stickers or glitter, or even by gluing dry decorations to it.
2. Use construction paper if foam paper is not available.

The Fall

Genesis 3

Memory Verse:
"Did God say that?"
(Genesis 3:1)

God told Adam and Eve that they could eat any of the delicious fruit in the Garden of Eden, except for the fruit of the tree of the knowledge of good and evil, which was in the middle of the garden. Adam and Eve were very happy in the garden. They were warm and comfortable. They had fresh cool water to drink and excellent food to eat. The weather was so perfect that they didn't even need to wear clothes. God had taken care of everything.

One day, Eve was walking alone in the garden. The serpent, a cunning creature, who was really the devil, tempted Eve. He said, "Did God really say not to eat this fruit?" Eve said, "We can eat of the fruit of any tree in the garden, except this one, lest we die." But the serpent said, "You will not die. But, when you eat this fruit, your eyes will be open and you will be like God." So, Eve disobeyed God and ate some fruit of the tree. She gave some to

Adam, who also disobeyed God and ate the forbidden fruit. Suddenly, their eyes were opened, and Adam and Eve saw that they were naked, and they were ashamed.

They heard the sound of God walking in the garden, and they hid from God. God called Adam, "Where are you?" Adam said, "I hid myself from you because I was naked and afraid." God asked, "Did you eat from the tree which I commanded you not to eat?" Adam said, "Eve gave me the forbidden fruit." God asked Eve, "What is this that you have done?" Eve said, "The serpent lied to me and I ate." This is how our first parents fell from God's grace.

Sin came into the world through Adam and Eve's disobedience to God. God cursed the serpent and made him crawl on his belly and eat dust. God promised that the seed of the woman, Jesus, the son of Mary, the new Eve would one day come, and crush the head of the serpent. The Virgin Mary's obedience to God would one day overturn Eve's disobedience.

Because Adam and Eve sinned, God drove them out of the Garden of Eden. God made Adam and Eve clothes out of animal skins, and Adam began to work the ground to grow his food. God placed an angel with a flaming sword at the entrance to the Garden of Eden, to guard the tree of life.

The devil still lies and tries to trick people. The serpent was jealous that God loved Adam and Eve so much and made them in His image and likeness. God gave you a guardian angel to watch over you and to help you to be obedient. When you are afraid or tempted to be bad, pray to your guardian angel to help you to be good. Your guardian angel will help you to be obedient to God, and to stay out of trouble.

Angel of God,

my guardian dear,

to whom God's love commits me here,

ever this day be at my side,

to light, to guard,

to rule, and guide.

Amen.

Angel of God,

my guardian dear,

to whom God's love

commits me here.

Ever this day

be at my side,

to light, to guard,

to rule, and guide.

Amen.

The Fall

This craft will make a guardian angel which the children can use when praying their guardian angel prayer "Angel of God".

Materials:
Light colored dessert paper plates (yellow, light blue...), white coffee filters, glittery pipe cleaners, white construction paper, crayons, stapler, tape, and scissors.

Preparation:
1. Cut one slit in the paper plates all the way to the center of the plate.
2. Create a cone shape with the cut paper plate and staple in place. The body of the angel should now be able to stand upright.
3. Cut small circles from the white construction paper to be used as the face.
4. Cut pipe cleaners in half.

Assembling:
1. Fold the coffee filter in 1/2" sections back and forth as if you were creating a fan. After folding, staple the center of the filter and fan out the two sides. This creates the wings of the angel.
2. Tape the wings to the back of the angel's body (by the stapled seam).
3. Draw a happy face on the small circle.
4. Create a halo out of the pipe cleaner simply by bending one end and making it into a circle.
5. Tape the halo to the back of the face of the angel. Then tape this to the angel's body. Secure it as best as possible with additional tape.

Other ideas:
1. For younger children, prepare the wings for them.
2. For older children, allow them to make the whole craft with your assistance.
3. Decorate the body of the angel with glitter glue, lace, or fancy ribbon.
4. Use paper doilies cut into triangles for the wings and if paper plates are not available, heavy stock construction paper can work just fine.
5. Copy the "Angel of God" prayer from the lesson book and tape it to the body of the angel.

Cain and Abel

Genesis 4

Memory Verse:
"If you do well, lift up your head."
(Genesis 4:7)

God told Adam and Eve to increase and multiply. God loved people so much that He wanted to fill the whole world with His children. Cain was the first little boy born to Adam and Eve. Soon, a brother, Abel, was born. They played together and then they grew up to be bigmen.

Cain farmed the land and grew delicious crops to eat. Abel was a shepherd and tended his flocks. Soon it was time for Cain and Abel to offer sacrifice to the Lord. God expects that we give Him the first, and best, portion of what we earn. After all, everything comes from God in the first place. It is only right that we thank God for His goodness, by giving something back to Him. Mommy and Daddy give some money at church on Sunday to thank God for providing for your family.

Abel brought his best firstling lamb to offer to the Lord as a sacrifice, while Cain brought some of his crops. God was very pleased with Abel's offering. Cain became very angry and jealous because God was so pleased with Abel.

God said, "Cain, why are you angry, and why do you look so sad? If you do well, lift up your head. If you don't do well, sin waits for you, but you must master sinful desire" (Genesis 4:7).

Cain asked Abel his brother to go out into the field. And when they went into the field, Cain killed Abel in his jealous fury. Cain thought that nobody had seen his evil deed, and now he would be rid of his brother Abel. But God said to Cain, "Where is Abel your brother?" Cain lied, "I don't know. Am I my brother's keeper?" (Genesis 4:9). God was so disappointed. God knew that Cain had killed his brother Abel.

The Lord asked Cain, "What have you done? The voice of your brother's blood is crying to me from the ground" (Genesis 4:10). Now Cain would be punished. He would become a fugitive and a wanderer on the earth.

Why was God angry? All life is precious in God's sight. God wants us to love one another. Even when people annoy us or are mean to us, God wants us to respond in love and patience. Do you have any brothers or sisters? Brothers and sisters are a blessing from the Lord. What can you do to show your brothers and your sisters that you love them and will be there for them?

When we quarrel with others, we must repent and ask forgiveness. Say, "I'm sorry. Will you please forgive me?" The person who was wronged says, "I forgive you." Then hug and make up. Also, we tell God that we are sorry in the Act of Contrition.

The Act of Contrition

O my God, I am heartily sorry for having offended You.

I detest all my sins

because I fear the loss of heaven and pains of hell,

but most of all because they offend You, my God,

Who are all good and deserving of all my love.

I firmly resolve, with the help of Your grace, to sin no more

and to avoid the near occasion of sin.

Amen.

THE ACT OF CONTRITION

O my God, I am heartily sorry

for having offended You.

I detest all my sins because

I fear the loss of heaven

and pains of hell,

but most of all because they offend

You, my God,

Who are all good and deserving

of all my love.

I firmly resolve with the help

of Your grace, to sin no more,

and to avoid the near

occasion of sin.

Amen.

Cain and Abel

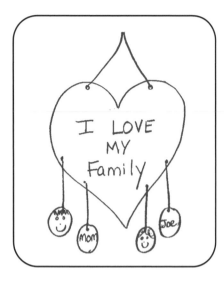

This craft will make a mobile, showing how much the children love their family.

Materials:
Pink foam paper, white construction paper, pencil, crayons, hole puncher, yarn, and scissors.

Preparation:
1. Trace and cut a large heart to use as a pattern. Fold a large piece of construction paper in half (short sides together) and trace half a heart, then cut.
2. Trace and cut a small circle (about 2" in diameter) to use as a pattern.
3. Cut pieces of yarn in 6" – 8" lengths.

Assembling:
1. Trace the heart pattern on pink foam paper. Cut it out.
2. Write "I Love My Family" in the heart with crayons or markers.
3. Trace the circle pattern on white construction paper. Trace as many circles as the child's family members and then cut them out.
4. Draw a picture of each family member's face on each circle and write their name on the back.
5. Punch a hole at the top of each white circle and then a hole along the lower edge of the heart (one for each family member). Attach the small circles to the heart using the cut pieces of yarn (simply by tying knots).
6. Punch two holes at the top of the heart to attach a longer piece of yarn so that the mobile can be hung up.

Other ideas:
1. For younger children, pre-cut the large heart and small circles for them.
2. Glue the family circles along the edge of the heart instead of using yarn.
3. Use construction paper for the whole craft.
4. Punch holes along the heart and let the children sew the edge of the heart with yarn and skip the "mobile" part.

Noah and the Ark

Genesis 6

Memory Verse:
**"Noah found favor in God's eyes"
(Genesis 6:8).**

Soon there were many families on the earth and many people. Some of the people were kind and good and loved God. Others were mean and evil and wicked. The bad people did terrible things, which made God very sad. "The Lord was sorry that He had made man on the earth, and it grieved His heart" (Genesis 6:6). God decided to blot out man from the face of the earth. "But, Noah found favor in the eyes of the Lord" (Genesis 6:8). Noah was a righteous man, a blameless man who walked with God. Noah had a wife and three sons, named Ham, Shem, and Japheth.

God told Noah His plan. "I have decided to make an end of mankind, for the earth is filled with violence" (Genesis 6:13). Then God told Noah to build a big ark, which is like a big house boat. God told Noah exactly how big to make it. The ark would have three decks and a roof on top. Noah obeyed God and did everything exactly as God told him. All the people in the neighborhood laughed at Noah. How foolish to build a big boat in your backyard where there is no water! Noah ignored the people laughing at him and making fun of him. Noah just kept on listening to God and obeying the voice of God.

When the ark was finished, God told Noah to bring two animals, a male and female of every kind of animal on earth. Noah found a boy giraffe and a girl giraffe. He found two lions, two donkeys, two cows, two pigs, and two monkeys. Ham, Shem, and Japheth helped their father build the ark and round up all the animals. They even found two puppies, two elephants, two rabbits, two hamsters, and two frogs. How many animals can you name for Noah to put in the ark? Which are your favorite animals?

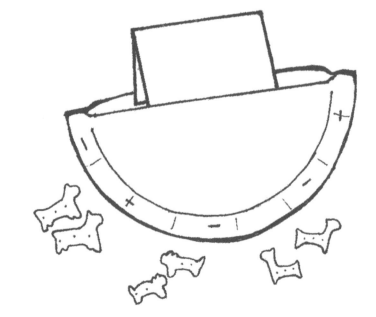

Noah and the Ark

The children will make an ark and fill it using animal crackers.

Materials:
White paper plates, brown construction paper, brown and black crayons or markers, scissors, stapler, glue, and animal crackers.

Preparation:
1. Fold and cut the paper plates in half.
2. Fold brown construction paper in half (short sides together) and then in half again (same way). Cut the paper along the seams to create rectangles (the top of the ark).

Assembling:
1. Color the outer side of two paper plates brown.
2. Staple or glue the two sides of the plates together along the circular edge. The "cut" edge should not be attached.
3. Fold the paper rectangle in half (short sides together) and draw windows on each side.
4. Glue the shorter edges of the folded rectangle in the inside center of each paper plate. This will create the peak of the ark.
5. Pick two of each kind of animal cracker and put them on the ark.

Other ideas:
1. Add Noah to the ark by drawing him in the window (step 3) or by coloring, cutting, and pasting him from the illustration in the lesson.
2. Use a harder stock plate to make a sturdier ark.
3. Paint the ark brown.
4. Add a ramp to the ark with a long rectangle and demonstrate how the animals boarded the ark.

The Flood

Genesis 7-9

Memory Verse:
"The rainbow is a sign of God's covenant."
(Genesis 9:13)

The Lord told Noah to go into the ark with his wife, his sons and their wives, and all of the animals they had gathered. Noah obeyed God exactly as God commanded him.

No sooner had Noah, his family, and all the animals gotten into the ark when it started to rain. God shut the door of the ark for Noah. And it rained, and it rained, and it rained, and it rained. Soon the water was up to the front doors. Then the waters came up to the windows. People in the neighborhood climbed on top of the rooftops. The same people who laughed at Noah and made fun of him were now crying and wishing they could get into the ark. It rained for forty days and forty nights. The whole earth was flooded with water.

The ark floated on the water. But all of the people and animals on the earth died in the flood. Only Noah, and those in the ark with him, were saved. The waters remained on the earth many days while Noah and his family floated around in the ark.

After a long time, the waters abated. Then the ark came to rest on Mount Ararat. After forty days, Noah opened the window of the ark and sent forth a raven. But the raven came back. Then Noah sent out a dove, but the dove found no place to set her foot so she returned. Noah put out his hand and brought the dove back into the ark. Noah waited another week and again he let the dove out. This time, the dove came back with an olive leaf in her mouth, so Noah knew that the flood had ended. Noah waited another seven days and let the dove out again. This time, the dove did not return to the ark.

God then told Noah to take his family and the animals, and leave the ark. Noah was so happy to be on dry ground again! He built an altar to the Lord in thanksgiving. God was pleased with Noah. God said, "Never again will I destroy every living thing as I have done. While the earth remains, seedtime and harvest, cold and heat, summer and winter, day and night shall not cease" (Genesis 8:21–22).

God blessed Noah and his family. He told them to be fruitful and multiply, and fill the earth. Then God made a beautiful rainbow in the sky with every color in it. The rainbow is a sign of God's covenant with Noah and all people after him. When you see a rainbow in the sky, remember God's covenant. God promises that He loves you and will be with you always. God will never abandon you, or forsake you. God loves you, all the time. Don't ever be afraid. God loves you with an everlasting love.

ACT OF HOPE

O my God,

relying on Your infinite

goodness and promises,

I hope to obtain

pardon for my sins,

the help of Your grace,

and life everlasting,

through the merits of

Jesus Christ,

my Lord and Redeemer.

The Flood

This craft will make a mosaic rainbow representing God's promise that He loves us and will be with us always.

Materials:
White paper plates, 4–5 colors of construction paper, scissors, glue sticks, pencil, and markers.

Preparation:
1. Fold and cut paper plates in half.
2. Cut tiny squares (1/2" x 1/2") of colored construction paper. Each craft will need approximately 30 squares of each color.

Assembling:
1. Select one color of tiny squares and glue them along the outer edge of the plate. This will create the outermost part of the rainbow.
2. Select the next color and glue them directly under the first row of the rainbow. Continue this step until all colors are used. The mosaic rainbow will be complete.
3. Finish the craft by writing "God's Promise" in the remaining space (underneath the rainbow).

Other ideas:
1. Punch a hole at the top of the finished project and hang the rainbow with yarn.
2. Use tiny crumpled colored tissue paper instead of construction paper.
3. Use white construction paper instead of the paper plates (cut a half circle to start the craft.
4. For younger children, draw the rainbow lines on the paper plate and allow them to color the rainbow, rather than using the glue.

The Tower of Babel

Genesis 11

Memory Verse:
"Come let us build a city and a tower to heaven."
(Genesis 11:4)

The whole world spoke one and the same language, and had few words. People moved from place to place, settling where they found the most pleasant land and the nicest views of water and trees.

One day, the people said to one another, "Come let us make bricks and burn them thoroughly. Let us build a city, and a tower with its top in the heavens, and let's make a name for ourselves, lest we be scattered abroad" (Genesis 11:3-4).

The people were filled with the sin of pride. They were not content with what God had given them to enjoy. They wanted more. They wanted to be like God. They wanted to make their own way to heaven, without God's help or invitation. They were pushy people. Do you know any pushy people who want to take things before they are offered to them? We don't want to be pushy people. We want to be pleasant people who are grateful for what we are given.

But the pushy people started to build their tower to heaven. God saw what the people were doing. So, God confused their language so that they could not understand one another. Then God scattered them abroad, all over the face of the earth. The tower they were building is called the Tower of Babel, because this is where their language was scrambled. Babble is like baby-talk. You can't understand what people say.

Later, the Holy Spirit came at Pentecost with tongues of fire, and people who spoke many different languages could understand one another. God is so good. God can confound the wise and instruct the simple. He can make humble people understand, and he can confuse the proud. Always be humble. Have expectant faith, and be thankful for everything that God provides for you.

Did you know that God provides a way for us to get to heaven? We don't need to build a tower. We just need Jesus.

The Tower of Babel

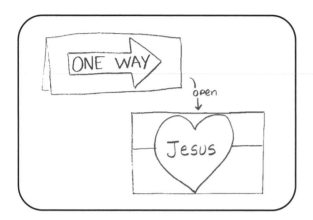

This craft will make a "One Way" sign, which, when opened, will show the way to heaven — JESUS!

Materials:
Black, white, and red construction paper, scissors, glue sticks, pencil, and crayons.

Preparation:
1. Fold (long sides together) and cut a piece of white construction paper in half. Then, trace and cut a pattern of a large thick arrow.
2. Trace and cut a pattern of a large heart from the red paper.

Assembling:
1. Using the pattern, have the children trace and cut a large white arrow.
2. Have the children write in big letters "One Way" on the arrow.
3. Fold the black construction paper in half (long sides together) and glue the one way sign on the top of the folded black paper.
4. Using the heart pattern, trace and cut a heart with red paper.
5. Open the one way sign.
6. Glue the heart in the middle of the black paper.
7. Write "Jesus" in the heart.

Other ideas:
1. For younger children, have the white arrows and hearts pre-cut for them to work with.
2. Use glitter and glue to write "Jesus" in the heart.
3. Emphasize to the children that a "One Way" sign shows us the ONLY way we should go, and that way is through JESUS.

God Calls Abram

Genesis 12-14

Memory Verse:
"I will make you a great nation.
I will bless you and make your name great."
(Genesis 12:2)

One day, God told a man called Abram to leave his country and go to a land that God would show him. God promised to be with Abram and make a great nation of his descendants. God would make Abram's name great and bless him and his family. Abram and his wife, Sarai, were very old, and sad because they didn't have any children or grandchildren.

What do you think Abram did? He told Sarai to pack up their belongings and get ready to move. Abram lived long ago, before there were planes, or trains, or automobiles. Abram and Sarai had to put their belongings on a donkey and walk to their new land. They would have to camp out at night under the stars, and look for water, and hunt for food along the way.

While on their journey, Abram looked out and saw some beautiful land with lush trees and running streams. God told

Abram to look at all the land as far as he could see, because this would be the land that God would give him.

God took care of Abram. He made sure that Abram and Sarai had enough food to eat, even when there was a famine in the land and other people were hungry. God made the Pharaoh of Egypt give presents to Abram and Sarai, even when Abram was not entirely honest with Pharaoh.

One day Melchizedek, king of Salem, brought bread and wine, and blessed Abram, saying, "Blessed be Abram by God Most High, maker of heaven and earth" (Genesis 14:19).

Abram was thankful that God was so good to him. Abram built an altar to God and gave one tenth of everything he had. Abram was grateful and generous. We want to be like Abram and say, "Thank you" when we receive a blessing. We also want to share what we have and return an offering to the Lord. Sing:

O, oh, oh how good is the Lord!
O, oh, oh how good is the Lord!
He gave me nice food, how good is the Lord!
He gave me my Mommy, how good is the Lord!
He gave me my Daddy, how good is the Lord!
I never will forget what He has done for me.

God Calls Abram

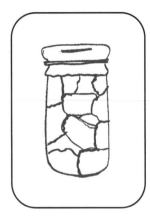

This craft will make an "Offering Bank" to use for saving, sharing, and offering to the Lord at church

Materials:
Large empty baby food jars, colorful tissue paper, felt, rubber bands, glue, paint brushes, and scissors.

Preparation:
1. Cut small (2"x 2") square pieces of colored tissue paper.

2. Cut felt circles (1 per craft) using a mug or glass as a pattern.

Assembling:
1. Brush on the glue to a section on the outside of the baby food jar. Then, place the square pieces of tissue paper over the applied glue.

2. Continue with step 1 until the jar is covered with the tissue paper.

3. Apply a finish coat of glue to give the bank a shiny look.

4. Fold the circle of felt in half and cut a small slit in the center about 1/2" long. When the circle is unfolded, the slit should be 1" to allow a quarter to pass through.

5. Place the felt over the top of the jar (slit over the opening) and use the rubber band to attach the felt to the jar (twisting the band around the lip of the jar).

Other ideas:
1. Use decorative napkins in place of tissue paper for a fancy look.

2. For younger children, cut larger pieces of tissue paper and apply the glue to the whole jar before attaching the tissue paper.

3. Use a thick dark marker and put their name and the word "Offering" on the bank (for example, "Emily's Offering").

God's Covenant with Abram

Genesis 15

Memory Verse:
"Fear not, I am your shield."
(Genesis 15:1)

God came to Abram in a vision, which is like God visiting you in a dream at night. The Lord said to Abram, "Fear not, Abram, I am your shield and your reward will be very great" (Genesis 15:1).

But Abram was sad because he was very old and still didn't have any children. Abram told God how sad he was. What good was it, to have blessings from God, if he had no son to pass on his inheritance? Abram thought that when he died, all his belongings would go to his servant Eliezer.

But God told Abram, "Eliezer shall not be your heir; your own son shall be your heir" (Genesis 15:4). God took Abram outside and said, "Look up to heaven, and count the stars in the sky. Your descendants will be as numerous as the stars in the sky" (Genesis 15:5-6). Abram believed everything that God told him, and God counted Abram a righteous man.

God made a covenant with Abram. A covenant is a promise that cannot be broken. Sometimes people make a promise, and then break it. But God cannot break His word.

Daddy might promise to take you swimming. But then it rains, and you can't go! But God knows the weather, the future, the past. God knows everything. Everything that God promises comes true! You can count on God. You can believe God.

That night when Abram was sleeping, God sent a flaming torch to pass through some birds that Abram had cut up. God showed that His covenant comes from heaven and depends on God alone, not on man. Even if man is unfaithful, God remains faithful to His word and His promise. We want to be true to our word, too. We believe God and trust in His word. We believe that God is good, all the time. He is a loving Father to us.

Our Father, who art in heaven, hallowed be Thy name,
Thy kingdom come, Thy will be done on earth as it is in heaven.
Give us this day our daily bread,
And forgive us our trespasses
as we forgive those who trespass against us,
And lead us not into temptation but deliver us from evil. Amen.

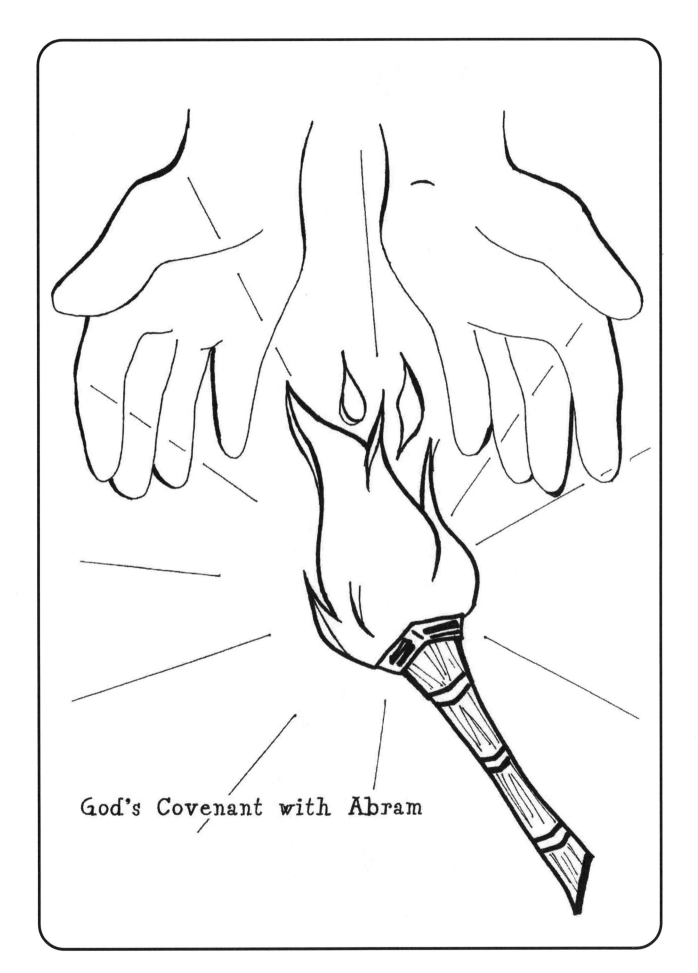

God's Covenant with Abram

The children will make a flaming torch like the one given to Abram by God.

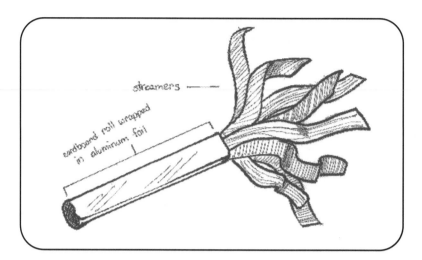

streamers

cardboard roll wrapped in aluminum foil

Materials:
Cardboard from paper towel rolls (1 per craft), aluminum foil, yellow and orange party streamers, scissors, and tape.

Preparation:
1. Pre-cut pieces of aluminum foil that will wrap around the towel roll.

Assembling:
1. Wrap aluminum foil around the paper towel roll and tape the seams at the end (tuck in any extra pieces into the tube ends).

2. Cut 6" pieces of yellow and orange party streamers.

3. Pinch together the tip of each streamer, then tuck the tip into the tube and tape it secure. Repeat this step until 3 – 4 yellow and orange streamers have been added.

4. Wave the torch around slightly to get the effect of a burning torch.

Other ideas:
1. Cut and add orange and yellow flame shapes to the torch for more "flaming" effect.

2. Use crumpled yellow and orange tissue paper.

The Birth of Ishmael

Genesis 16

Memory Verse:
"The Lord has heard your cry."
(Genesis 16:11)

Ten years passed. Now Abram was very old, and still he and Sarai had no children. They were sad and lonely. They were getting older and older. Abram and Sarai were older than your grandparents and yet they had no children. They had never enjoyed the laughter of little children in their home. They couldn't hear a baby cry or listen for the pitter-patter of little feet.

Sarai got tired of waiting on God. She decided to take matters into her own hands. Sarai told Abram, "The Lord has prevented me from bearing children; go in to my maid; it may be that I shall get children by her" (Genesis 16:2). This was a very bad idea! God wants husbands and wives to be faithful to one another, whether He blesses them with children or not.

Abram did as Sarai suggested and had a baby with the maid, Hagar. When Sarai saw that Hagar was pregnant, she became very angry and mistreated Hagar. Soon, the whole household was in an uproar, and Hagar ran away.

Hagar ran away into the wilderness and started to cry. She was hungry, thirsty, cold, and tired. Sarai was mean to Hagar, and nobody wanted her. Hagar just cried and cried.

Soon an angel of the Lord found Hagar and asked where she was going. Hagar told the angel that she was fleeing from her mistress, Sarai. The angel told Hagar to go back to Sarai and be obedient to her. The angel also told Hagar that the baby she was carrying would be a boy. "You should call his name Ishmael, because the Lord has heard your cry" (Genesis 16:11).

The angel told Hagar that Ishmael would be a wild man, and everyone would want to fight with him. But God would also give many descendants to Ishmael.

Hagar knew that the Lord had sent the angel to speak to her, and she believed in God. She obeyed the angel and went back home to Sarai and Abram. Hagar's son, Ishmael, was born when Abram was eighty-six years old. Sometimes, we might think we have a good idea. But it is important to pray first and ask God.

The Birth of Ishmael

Craft — The Birth of Ishmael

The craft will make a little baby Ishmael and a little blanket for the baby.

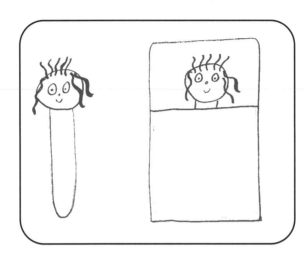 

Materials:
Felt, craft sticks, construction paper, yarn, crayons, glue, and scissors.

Preparation:
1. Trace and cut a pattern of a medium circle.
2. Cut small pieces of yarn for hair.
3. Cut felt into large rectangles. For each square piece of felt, fold and cut in half.

Assembling:
1. Fold the shorter side of the felt in about 2" from the other end. This will form the blanket. Glue the longer edges together. Be careful NOT to glue the shorter end of the felt. This will allow the craft stick to slide into the blanket.
2. Trace and cut the baby's head by using the circle pattern on construction paper.
3. Draw a face on the circle using crayons.
4. Glue the face onto an end of a craft stick.
5. Glue yarn on the head to create hair.
6. Place baby Ishmael into his bed.

Other ideas:
1. Create a baby using a roasted peanut (in the shell), and glue tiny eyes to it.
2. Create a baby using a wooden ice-cream spoon and draw a face on it.
3. Use material or foam paper to replace the felt.
4. Glue cut copies of the Bible verse to the front of the blanket.

Sodom and Gomorrah

Genesis 17-19

Memory Verse:
"Why did Sarah laugh?"
(Genesis 18:13)

When Abram was ninety-nine years old, he and Sarai still had no children. God appeared to Abram again and repeated His promise. God changed Abram's name to Abraham, and Sarai's name to Sarah. God told Abraham to always love God and to keep His covenant, along with his children and grandchildren.

God told Abraham He would give Sarah a son. Abraham fell on his face and laughed. Could a baby be born to a one hundred year-old man? Could an old lady like Sarah give birth to a baby?

Three men came to Sarah and Abraham's house. Abraham asked Sarah to make cakes for the visitors and give them something to eat. The Lord said, "I will come back in the spring and Sarah will have a son" (Genesis 18:9). Sarah was listening in the kitchen, and she started to laugh.

Then, the Lord told Abraham that the wicked people in Sodom and Gomorrah were doing very bad things. God planned to destroy the city. But Abraham bargained with God. "What if there are fifty good people there? Will you still destroy it?"(Genesis 19:24). God promised that He would spare the city if there were fifty good people. "What if there are only forty good people?" asked Abraham. God agreed to spare the city if there were forty righteous people. "If there are thirty, would you spare it?" asked Abraham. God agreed. "What if there are only twenty good people, or even ten nice people?" God agreed not to destroy the bad city, if there were even ten righteous people.

But, there were not even ten good people. So angels went to get Lot, Abraham's nephew, and his family out of danger. "Get out quickly and don't look back," the angels said. So, Lot and his wife and children ran from the city, just as the Lord rained fire from heaven on the city. Lot's wife looked back and became a pillar of salt. But, Lot and his children were safe. When God tells you there is danger, listen to Him. Obey God, don't hesitate, and don't look back!

Sodom and Gomorrah

The children will use clay to mold a model of Lot's wife as a pillar of salt.

Materials:
Modeling clay and wax paper.

Assembling:
1. Place a sheet of wax paper in front of each child to create a workspace.

2. Create a person out of the clay. The easiest way to do this is to make a ball out of dough and place it on top of another ball of dough (like a snowman). Then add small pieces of dough to create the face.

Other ideas:
1. Use clay tools like plastic knives (to cut), small dowels (to roll), and even tiny shape cutters to decorate Lot's wife.

2. Older children may use different colors of clay to be creative.

The Birth of Isaac~The Test

Genesis 21-22

Memory Verse:
"God Himself will provide."
(Genesis 22:8)

When Abraham and Sarah were very, very old, God fulfilled His promise and sent them a son, Isaac. Abraham and Sarah were so happy. Now, there was a baby in their house. Now there would be love and laughter and joy.

One day, Isaac and Ishmael, his half-brother, were playing. Sarah got mad, and sent Hagar and Ishmael away. Once again, Hagar ran into the wilderness with Ishmael. Once again, God watched over them and protected them.

After a time, God tested Abraham to see how much he loved God. God asked Abraham to take his son, Isaac, whom he loved, to the land of Moriah, to offer him as a burnt offering to God. Now, the pagans would offer their children in sacrifice, but all life is precious to God. So, this didn't make sense! Nevertheless, Abraham obeyed God.

Abraham got up early in the morning and took Isaac, two servants, and cut wood for the offering. After traveling for three days, Abraham saw Mount Moriah and told his servants to remain behind. Abraham and Isaac journeyed on alone. Abraham put the wood for the burnt offering on Isaac's shoulders, while he took the fire and the knife himself.

Isaac said, "Father, here is the fire and the wood, but where is the lamb for sacrifice?" Abraham said, "God Himself will provide" (Genesis 22:7-8).

When they got to the place, Abraham built an altar, put the wood on the altar, and prepared to sacrifice his beloved son, Isaac. But an angel of the Lord stopped Abraham from harming his son. God saw that Abraham would not keep anything from the Lord. Abraham saw a ram caught in a thicket by its horns, and offered that ram to the Lord.

God was pleased with Abraham's willingness to offer everything to God, even his only son, whom he loved. Because Abraham loved God so much, God promised to bless Abraham.

What is most precious to you? Could you give it to God?

The Birth of Isaac- The Test

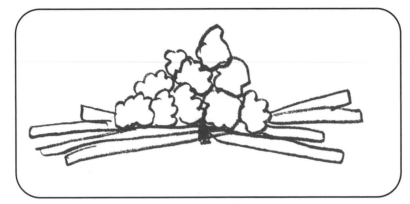

The craft will make a pretend fire like the one Abraham made on the mountain.

Materials:
Thin sticks (twigs), bag ties, yellow and orange tissue paper, and glue.

Preparation:
1. Collect thin sticks and break them into 6"–8" pieces.

Assembling:
1. Tie about 4 to 6 sticks together in the center using the bag tie.

2. Make sure the twigs are secure and wiggle them a little bit apart to create the look of wood used in a fireplace.

3. Crumple small pieces of orange and yellow tissue paper and glue each piece in the center of the sticks (over the area with the tie).

4. Continue to glue the orange and yellow tissue paper in a pile to create the "fire."

Other ideas:
1. Use black pipe cleaners if bag ties aren't available.

Isaac and Rebekah

Genesis 24

Memory Verse:
"O Lord, give me success today."
(Genesis 24:12)

When Abraham was very, very old, and Isaac was all grown up, Abraham called his chief servant and said, "Promise me that you won't find a wife for my son Isaac from among the pagans, but go back to my country, and find him a wife from among my kinsmen." But the servant asked, "What if the woman won't come to this land?" Abraham told his servant that if the woman didn't want to come, the servant would be free from his promise.

So the servant did as Abraham asked, and traveled back to the city of Nahor. On arrival, he had the camel kneel down by the well of water. And he prayed, "O Lord, God of my master Abraham, give me success today and show steadfast love to Abraham. Let a woman come and offer me a drink as a sign that this is the woman you have chosen for Isaac."

Before the servant had finished speaking, Rebekah, one of

Abraham's relatives, came out with a water jar on her shoulder. Rebekah was very beautiful and had never been married. She went to the spring and filled her jar with water. The servant asked Rebekah for a drink. She gave the servant a drink and then gave the camels a drink, too. They were all very thirsty.

The servant asked Rebekah whose daughter she was and if there was room in her father's house for him to spend the night. Rebekah invited the traveler to come to her house and bring his camels to where the straw was stored.

The servant said, "Blessed be the Lord, the God of Abraham for the love and faithfulness He has shown" (Genesis 24:26).

Rebekah went home and told her brother Laban all about the man at the well. The servant explained to her family how God had led him to Rebekah when he prayed for a wife for Isaac. Rebekah agreed to go back with the servant to marry Isaac, love him, and be a good wife to him.

When the servant and Rebekah came back home, Isaac was working in the field. He looked up and saw Rebekah and fell in love with her. Rebekah saw Isaac and she loved him, too.

Wasn't this an amazing way for God to bring two people together in marriage? When you grow up, God might call you to be married, or He might call you to be a priest, brother, or sister. Whatever your vocation is, start praying about it right now. Sometimes young boys, as young as you, hear God calling them to serve Him as holy priests of God. Holy Mother Church needs good priests, and if God calls you, pray that you will be a holy priest. And if God calls you to the married life, pray that you will be a good husband or wife. Pray that God will show you the perfect spouse that He has prepared for you from the beginning of time.

Take Lord, receive all my benefits,

my memory, my understanding, my entire will.

Your grace and Your love are enough for me.

Give me these, Lord, and I ask for nothing more.

Amen.

Father, Yours is the harvest and Yours is the Vineyard.

You assign the task and pay a wage that is just.

Help me to be faithful in all my responsibilities today,

and never let me be separated from You.

Prayer for Vocations

Father God, thank you for blessing us with a wonderful family. Watch over us and help us to love one another always. Thank you for blessing our Church family with priests and religious sisters and brothers. They help us to live according to Your Word. Bless and strengthen them Lord.

Dear God, please send more men and women to serve You and Your Church. We pray that, if it is Your will, members of our own family will hear and answer Your call to serve You as a priest, religious sister, or brother, so that generations to come will continue to share in the joy we know in You.

Craft — Isaac and Rebekah

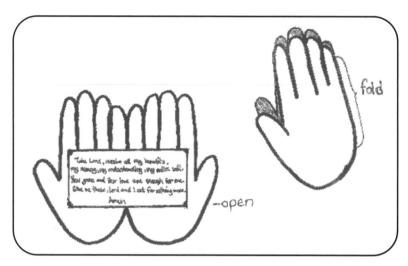

The children will make praying hands that, when opened, will show the prayer from the lesson.

Materials:
Colored construction paper, prayer from the lesson, scissors, pencil, glue, and decorative items (glitter, stickers, etc.).

Preparation:
1. Copy the prayer from the "Isaac and Rebekah" lesson (one per craft needed).

Assembling:
1. Fold construction paper (short sides together).
2. Place left hand on paper with the pinky on the edge of the fold. Trace the hand and cut. Be careful not to cut the folded edge.
3. Cut out the copy of the prayer along the border.
4. Open the praying hands and glue the prayer to the inside.
5. Finish decorating the outside of the praying hands with crayons, glitter glue or stickers.
6. Stand the praying hands up and pray the wonderful prayer!

Other ideas:
1. For younger children, a hand pattern may need to be provided in place of step 2.

Jacob and Esau

Genesis 25-27

Memory Verse:
**"May God give you the dew of heaven
and the richness of earth."
(Genesis 27:28)**

Isaac and Rebekah married and had twin sons. Esau was born first and had ruddy skin. Jacob, holding his brother's heel, was born soon after. When they grew up, Esau was a skillful hunter. Jacob, a quiet man, lived in a tent. Isaac loved Esau, because Esau would hunt good food. Rebekah favored Jacob.

One day Jacob was cooking lentil stew. Esau came in and was very hungry. Esau wanted to eat some of Jacob's stew. But Jacob said, "First sell me your birthright." Because Esau was the first-born son, he was entitled to the biggest portion of family land and blessing, but he didn't care very much about it. So, he gave away his birthright to Jacob for bean soup: lentil stew!

When Esau was forty years old, he married Judith, one of the pagan women, which made his mother Rebekah very upset. Rebekah wanted her sons to marry women who loved God.

When Isaac was old and close to death, he called Esau. Isaac asked Esau to go hunt some game and prepare a tasty dish for him. Then Isaac would give Esau his blessing.

Rebekah heard Isaac and decided to trick her husband. She prepared some food for Jacob to give to Isaac. She put furry gloves on Jacob, so his skin would feel like Esau's. Isaac was now old and almost blind. When Jacob brought the food, Isaac was surprised that Esau was back so soon. When asked how he got back so quickly, Jacob said, "The Lord granted me success."

Isaac thought something was fishy. He felt the hands that felt like Esau's, but the voice was Jacob's. When he had eaten, Isaac gave Jacob his blessing.

Soon, Esau came home with the game he had caught, and brought it to his father. Isaac told him that he had already eaten. But who had brought that food? Jacob had tricked his father, Isaac, and he had received the blessing.

Esau was so mad! "Father, did you give my blessing to my brother, Jacob? Don't you have a blessing for me, too?" asked Esau. Isaac told Esau that he had given Jacob the blessing that was reserved for the firstborn son, the birthright blessing.

Now Rebekah could see that Esau was mad enough to kill Jacob. So, she told Isaac that she wanted to send Jacob away to find a wife from among the God-fearing women. Jacob thought it was a good idea to get out of town for awhile, until Esau could cool off and stop being so mad at him. So, Jacob kissed his father and mother, Isaac and Rebekah, good-bye and left to go to the country of his mother's family.

Do you know that you have a mother in heaven who always watches over you? Our Blessed Mother, Mary, is the mother of Jesus. When Jesus died on the Cross, He gave His mother to all the people who love Him. If you are all alone, or afraid, or if you can't find your Mommy, you can pray to Our Blessed Mother. She will comfort you and take care of you. Mary loves you very much. She invites you to come to her with your needs.

Hail Mary

Hail Mary, full of grace,
the Lord is with thee.
Blessed are thou among women
and blessed is the fruit of thy womb, Jesus.
Holy Mary, Mother of God,
pray for us sinners,
now and at the hour of our death. Amen.

HAIL MARY

Hail Mary, full of grace,

the Lord is with thee.

Blessed are thou among women

and blessed is the fruit

of thy womb, Jesus.

Holy Mary, Mother of God,

pray for us sinners,

now and at the hour

of our death.

Amen.

Esau and Jacob

The craft will make a pot of stew similar to the one Jacob and Rebekah made.

Materials:
Construction paper, dry beans (lentil, black, etc.), plastic spoons, pencils, glue, and scissors.

Preparation:
1. Trace and cut a pattern of a pot with a handle.

Assembling:
1. Trace and cut a pot using the pattern on dark construction paper.

2. Glue the "pot" onto a new piece of construction paper.

3. Glue dry beans over the top of the pot to form the lentil stew.

4. Glue a plastic spoon in the "stew."

Other ideas:
1. Bring in a real pot of lentil or bean stew and let the children snack on this after making the craft.

2. Other dry stew items could include: dry peas, dry corn (popcorn kernels), pumpkin seeds, cereal, or even jelly beans.

Jacob's Ladder

Genesis 28

Memory Verse:
"Surely the Lord is in this place."
(Genesis 28:16)

Jacob left home and set out for Haran, the place where his mother Rebekah's family lived. Esau was still fuming mad at Jacob for taking his birthright by trickery. But when you trick and deceive others, sometimes you will be fooled as well.

Nighttime came, and Jacob was tired. He used a stone for a pillow, and lay down to sleep. Jacob had a dream. In his dream, a stairway reached from heaven to earth, and angels of God were ascending and descending. At the top of the ladder in heaven stood the Lord, and He said, "I am the Lord, the God of your fathers Abraham and Isaac. I will give you the land on which you are lying. You will have many children. All the people on earth will be blessed by you. I am with you and will watch over you wherever you go, and I will bring you back to this land. I will not leave you until I have done everything I promised."

When Jacob woke up in the morning, he said, "Surely the Lord is in this place" (Genesis 28:16). Jacob said, "How awesome is this place! This is none other than the house of God, and this is the gate of heaven" (Genesis 28:17).

So Jacob took the stone he had been using for a pillow, poured oil on it, and made a pillar for God. He named that place Bethel, which means "house of God."

Jacob decided that if God would be with him on his journey and watch over him and provide food to eat so that he could return to his father's home in peace, then the Lord would be his God too. Jacob would worship the living God, and Jacob would give to God one-tenth of all that he was given.

The angels on Jacob's ladder show us that God provides a way for us to get to heaven. What do you think heaven will be like?

Your parents had you baptized, so that you can go to heaven. Ask your guardian angel to help you to stay in the state of grace, so that you can go to heaven and see Jesus one day.

Jacob's Ladder

The children can build a "noodle" ladder similar to the one in Jacob's dream.

Materials:
Colorful foam paper, uncooked ziti noodles, white paper, crayons, scissors, and glue.

Assembling:
1. Write "Heaven" at the top of the paper with a cloud around it.
2. Trace and cut the shape of a rock using white paper and write "Bethel" on it. This was Jacob's pillow. Glue it to the bottom of the page.
3. Begin gluing pasta to the page to create the ladder. Start from the bottom and glue the ladder steps onto the page. Then add the noodles to create the sides of the ladder.

Other ideas:
1. For younger children, use the glue and draw the ladder onto the page. Then let the children stick the noodles onto the paper.
2. Use tri-colored pasta for a colorful ladder.
3. Use fettuccini noodles for the longer part of the ladder and break up the fettuccini noodles for the ladder steps.

Laban Tricks Jacob

Genesis 29

Memory Verse:
**"Lead me in truth and teach me,
for You are the God of my salvation."
(Psalm 25:5)**

Jacob came to a well in the field, and flocks of sheep gathered around the well. Jacob learned that the shepherds were from Haran. He asked about his mother Rebekah's brother, Laban. The shepherds told Jacob that Laban was alive and well. "Here comes Laban's daughter, Rachel, with his sheep right now," said the shepherds.

When Jacob saw Rachel, he helped to move the stone from the well, so she could water her father's sheep. Rachel was very beautiful, and Jacob fell in love with her. When Jacob told Rachel that he was Laban's relative, she ran to tell her father.

Laban was happy to see Jacob. Laban said, "Surely you are my bone and my flesh." That means that they were related to each other. They were in the same big family.

Jacob asked Laban for permission to marry his daughter

Rachel. Laban gave his permission, but told Jacob that he would have to work for seven years, caring for the sheep, in order to marry Rachel. Jacob was so in love that he was happy to work with the sheep in order to marry Rachel.

Soon the wedding day came. In that place, a bride would wear a heavy veil over her face on her wedding day. Jacob promised to love, honor, and care for his wife. Do you know what happened? Laban tricked Jacob. Jacob was deceived. Under the veil was Leah, the sister of Rachel, not Rachel! Just like Jacob had tricked Esau, now Laban tricked Jacob. Jacob didn't think that was funny at all.

In those days, before Jesus came, sometimes a man would marry more than one woman. So Jacob worked another seven years, and married both Rachel and her sister, Leah. God blessed Jacob with twelve sons named Reuben, Simeon, Levi, Judah, Dan, Napthali, Gad, Asher, Issachar, Zebulun, Joseph, and Benjamin. How many children are in your family? What are the names of your brothers and sisters? Pray that God will help you to always be honest and to tell the truth.

Laban Tricks Jacob

Craft — Laban Tricks Jacob

The children will make a coloring booklet using the illustration from the lesson.

Materials:
Copies of the lesson's illustration, crayons or markers, construction paper, and glue sticks.

Preparation:
1. Copy the illustration from the lesson.

Assembling:
1. Color the illustration using crayons or markers.

2. Glue the coloring page to a piece of construction paper using the glue stick.

Other ideas:
1. Create a "Jacob" coloring booklet by copying all the Jacob illustrations, gluing them to construction paper and then stapling them together. As each lesson is taught, allow the child to color a page, which will help reinforce the story.

Jacob Goes Home

Genesis 31-33

Memory Verse:
"The God of my father is with me."
(Genesis 31:5)

Jacob was homesick. He had lived in Haran for many years. Laban kept playing tricks on Jacob and deceiving him. Laban kept changing Jacob's wages. Always tell the truth. Always honor your word. When you agree to do something, do it. When you agree to pay a sum of money, pay the fair amount. Now, Jacob could see that it wasn't any fun to have someone trick him and lie to him. Jacob wanted to go home.

Jacob gathered Rachel, Leah, all of his children, and his livestock and started walking back home. They didn't tell Laban that they were leaving. When Laban found out that Jacob had left, he was mad. He chased after Jacob and caught up with him. Laban wanted to know why Jacob didn't say good-bye. In a dream, God told Laban to let Jacob go. So Laban kissed his daughters and grandchildren good-bye.

Twenty years had passed since Jacob had left home. Would Esau still be mad? Jacob had tricked Esau, but they were still brothers. Jacob was afraid that Esau would be still angry.

Jacob sent a present to Esau. Esau came running to see Jacob, and they were so happy to see one another after all these years. They cried happy tears. Jacob and Esau were brothers who loved one another. Jacob said that to see his brother again was like seeing the face of God!

So Jacob returned home to his father, Isaac. On the way home, God changed Jacob's name to Israel. Israel remembered that God had been with him, watching over him all those years. So he built a pillar at Bethel to thank God. Jacob remembered to thank God! Do you always remember to say "thank you?" If God changed your name, what would you like it to be? If you quarreled with your brother or sister and they asked forgiveness, would you be eager to forgive and make up?

How many things can you think of to thank God for? *Thank you, God, for Mommy and Daddy, and flowers and trees, and food and clothes, and toys and _____ .*

Jacob Goes Home

The craft will make "thankful tree" showing what each child is thankful to God for.

Materials:
Brown, red, yellow, orange, and white construction paper, pencil, marker, glue sticks, and scissors.

Preparation:
1. Trace and cut a leaf shape to be used as a pattern. An oval-like shape or maple leaf shape works best.

Assembling:
1. Create the tree trunk and branches by placing the child's elbow a little bit below the bottom of the brown construction paper (at the shorter end) and laying his hand down on the paper with his fingers spread open (to create the branches). Trace and cut.
2. Glue the tree trunk onto white construction paper.
3. Use the leaf pattern and trace at least two on red, yellow, and orange paper. Cut out the leaves.
4. Assist each child and write something he is thankful for on each leaf (God, Mommy, Daddy...) using the markers.
5. Glue each leaf at the end of the branches. 6. Write "Thank You God For..." at the top of the craft.

Other ideas:
1. Use fall colors for the leaves if craft is done in the fall or use shades of green to make the leaves in the spring and summer.
2. For younger children, pre-cut leaf shapes.
3. For younger children, trace their "tree trunk" onto brown construction paper with black marker and eliminate the cutting and gluing part of the tree trunk.
4. Use foam paper instead of construction paper.
5. Make a thankful "flower" garden. Trace and cut the child's handprint to use as tulip flowers and add stems and grass (or put them into a vase-like shape). Write what the child is thankful for on each flower.

Joseph the Dreamer

Genesis 37

Memory Verse:
**"Israel loved Joseph
more than any other of his children."
(Genesis 37:3)**

Joseph was the second youngest of the sons of Israel, and his father's favorite. Israel loved Joseph more than any of his other children, because Joseph was the son of his old age. One day, Israel made a beautiful coat of many colors with long sleeves for Joseph. Joseph put the coat on, and his brothers were so jealous, they couldn't even speak nicely to him.

Joseph was a dreamer. He would dream dreams at night and then tell his whole family about them. Once, Joseph dreamed that he and his brothers were binding wheat in the fields. Joseph's sheaf stood up straight, while his brother's sheaves bowed down to Joseph's. "Are you going to be boss over all of us?" asked his brothers. Now they were even madder at Joseph.

Another time, Joseph dreamed that the sun, the moon, and eleven stars bowed down to him. This was too much! Now, Israel, his father, scolded Joseph. "What is this dream? Will your mother and I, and your brothers, bow down to you?"

One day, Israel sent Joseph out to his brothers, who were tending their sheep. "Here comes that dreamer now," said his brothers. "Let's kill him and get rid of him." But Reuben said, "We must not shed his blood. Let's put him in a deep pit and think of something to do with him."

Later that day, some travelers on camels passed by on their way to Egypt. Judah said, "Let's sell Joseph to these Ishmaelites and not kill him, for he is our own brother." So the brothers sold Joseph into slavery. They took his beautiful coat of many colors, and put blood on it. When they went home, they showed the blood-stained robe to Israel and pretended that Joseph had been eaten by a wolf. Israel cried and cried for the loss of his son Joseph. He was so sad. He could not be consoled.

Wasn't that a mean thing that Joseph's brothers did to him? How would you have consoled Israel in his grief? What can you do to try to comfort someone who is sad?

Joseph the Dreamer

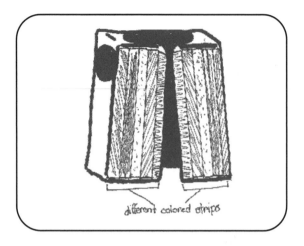

different colored strips

This craft will make a colorful coat the children can wear just like the coat that Joseph wore.

Materials:
Brown paper grocery bags, colored construction paper, pencil, glue, and scissors.

Preparation:
1. Trace and cut long rectangular strips of colorful construction paper. This can be done by using a straight edge and drawing lines on the construction paper (parallel to the long edge) about 2" apart.
2. Cut some of the strips in half. These will be used to decorate the front of the coat.
3. Cut the bag to look like a vest. First, turn the bag upside down and cut a slit in the center of the bag all the way to the top. Continue cutting a large circle in the small rectangular area where the groceries usually sit. This will be where the neck will go. Finally cut circles in the side rectangular section of the bag close to the top (the arms will go through here).

Assembling:
1. Glue the long strips of construction paper on the back of the vest and cut off any excess paper.
2. Glue the shorter strips of construction paper on the front, cutting off any excess paper. Allow the children to be creative with their color selection.

Other ideas:
1. Younger children can color the coat with crayons.
2. Paint the coat with lots of colors.
3. Use scraps of colorful and fancy material for decorating the coat.

Joseph in Prison

Genesis 39–40

Memory Verse:
**"The Lord was with Joseph,
and he became a successful man."
(Genesis 39:2)**

Joseph went to Egypt and became a successful servant in the home of Potiphar, an officer of Pharaoh. Potiphar trusted Joseph with taking care of his whole house.

Now Joseph grew into a handsome man. One day Potiphar's wife noticed how handsome Joseph was, and desired him. But Joseph ignored her. How could Joseph be so wicked as to sin against God? Potiphar's wife was angry that Joseph rejected her, and she told her husband a lie. She betrayed Joseph, saying he tried to force himself on her. Joseph was put into prison because of this lie. But God was still with Joseph.

Two prisoners, Pharaoh's butler and baker, had dreams which they told Joseph. In the butler's dream, he was holding Pharaoh's cup. There were grapes on a vine, which he squeezed, making wine in Pharaoh's cup. Joseph interpreted the dream for the butler. "In three days time, you will be restored to your former job as butler for Pharaoh." The butler was so happy. He promised to remember Joseph when he got out of prison.

The baker dreamed that birds were eating food out of three baskets that he was carrying on his head. Joseph said, "In three days Pharaoh will lift up your head and hang you from a tree."

In three days, on Pharaoh's birthday, he restored the butler to his position, but hanged the baker, just as Joseph had foretold. The chief butler was so happy to be out of prison and so excited to have his job back that he forgot all about Joseph. Poor Joseph was left in prison, even though he had done nothing wrong.

Sometimes people get punished for things that they didn't do. But don't worry. God knows the truth. In the end, God will punish the wicked and reward the righteous. We must always try to do the right thing. We know that God sees the heart, and knows when we are trying to do good. In the end, time will tell. God will judge. What can you do to be very, very good? What should you do if you are punished unfairly?

Joseph in Prison

Activity — Joseph in Prison

The children will play a singing game locking each other up in prison.

Materials:
None.

Preparation:
1. Teach the children the following song, singing it to the tune of "London Bridge is Falling Down":

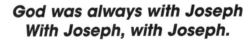

> ***"Joseph went to prison,***
> ***prison, prison.***
>
> ***Joseph went to prison,***
> ***Poor young Joseph.***
>
> ***God was always with Joseph***
> ***With Joseph, with Joseph.***
>
> ***God was always with Joseph***
> ***Hurray for Joseph!"***

Assembling:
1. Line the children up and have two children lock hands and place them up high like in "London Bridge" (they are the "prison").
2. Sing the song and let the children go under the prison to see who will be Joseph. When you start singing the part "God was always with Joseph" have the two children bring their arms down and lock Joseph up.
3. Take turns being the prison and of course allow all children to play the part of Joseph.

Other ideas:
1. For older children, allow them to make a prison out of blocks.

Pharaoh's Dream

Genesis 41

Memory Verse:
"God has made me forget my hardship."
(Genesis 41:51)

After two whole years, Pharaoh had a bad dream. He dreamed that he was standing by the Nile River, and seven fat, sleek cows came to eat the reed grass. Then, another seven skinny, sickly cows came and ate up the fat cows.

Pharaoh had a second dream. Seven plump good ears of grain were growing on one stalk. Then seven thin ears swallowed up the fat ears of grain. What did this mean? Pharaoh woke up in the morning very troubled by these bad dreams. No one could help Pharaoh to interpret and understand his dreams.

Just then, the butler remembered that when he was in prison, Joseph interpreted his dream and told the butler that he would be restored to his old job. Pharaoh called for Joseph to be brought out of the dungeon, and asked Joseph if he could interpret dreams. Joseph said, "I can't do it, but God will give the answer."

Joseph told Pharaoh that the seven fat cows meant seven years of plenty were coming followed by seven years of hunger and famine, when no crops would grow. The seven stalks of grain meant the same thing. There would be seven years of good crops followed by seven years when the ground would not produce food. Joseph told Pharaoh to get ready for hard times.

Pharaoh said, "Can we find such a man as this, who has the Spirit of God" (Genesis 41:38)? So Pharaoh said, "Since God has shown you all this, there is no one as wise as you are; you will be over my house. You will command my people what to do. Only on my throne will I be greater than you" (Genesis 41:39). Pharaoh put a beautiful robe, and a gold neck chain on Joseph.

Joseph harvested all the grain into big barns, storing up the food for the lean years. Joseph married and had two sons, Ephraim and Manasseh. God allowed Joseph to forget all the hardships he had faced. God made Joseph fruitful in the land of his affliction.

Do you see how God brought Joseph out of prison and into the palace? God is a good God all the time.

Pharaoh's Dream

Craft — Pharaoh's Dream

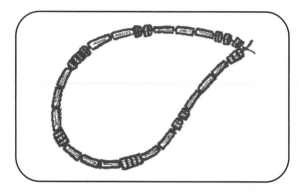

The children will make a gold neck chain like the one Pharaoh gave to Joseph for interpreting his dream.

Materials:
Ziti and wagon wheel noodles, newspaper, gold spray paint, string, and scissors.

Preparation:
1. Spray paint the noodles gold. First, spread the dry noodles over newspaper and spray paint (best to do this outside). Then, turn over the noodles and spray the other side.

Assembling:
1. Cut the string into 20" – 24" pieces. Tie a knot at one end of the string (you may need to tie multiple knots so the noodles don't slip off the end).

2. Put gold noodles onto string. Allow the children to be creative in selecting a pattern for their noodle beads.

3. Tie the string's ends together to make the necklace. Now, the children can wear their gold necklaces.

Other ideas:
1. Make a yellow paper-chain necklace. Cut rectangular strips of yellow construction paper (1"x4") and let the children glue each link together to create a necklace.

2. Bring in a fancy robe from home and let the children act out Pharaoh giving Joseph the fancy robe and gold necklace.

Joseph Saves His Family

Genesis 42-45

Memory Verse:
"God sent me before you to preserve life."
(Genesis 45:5)

Seven years of plenty came, followed by seven years of famine. Everyone was hungry, all over the whole earth. People came to Egypt from all over the world to find bread. Pharaoh told the people to go to Joseph and to do what he said.

Israel and his sons were hungry. Israel sent his sons to Egypt to buy food. But he did not let Benjamin go. When they arrived in Egypt, the brothers bowed before Joseph, just as the dream had foretold. Joseph recognized his brothers, but they did not recognize Joseph. Joseph asked about his father, Israel. The brothers told Joseph that Israel was alive and well, and at home with their youngest brother. Joseph accused them of being spies. He gave them food, but told them not to come back unless Benjamin came with them. Reuben said, "Now we are being punished by God for what we did to our brother Joseph so many years ago."

When the brothers got home, they gave the food to their families. They told their father that the man thought they were spies. They couldn't go back to Egypt without Benjamin.

Soon, they ran out of food again. Israel did not want to let Benjamin go with them, but they were so hungry. When the brothers returned to Egypt, Joseph met them again. He made a big feast, and gave Benjamin much more food! When Joseph saw Benjamin, he went out of the room and cried.

The brothers ate their meal, bought some food, and started to return home. Joseph had played a trick on them. He hid a silver cup in Benjamin's sack. When the brothers were not far from the palace, soldiers came to arrest them for robbery. "We are not robbers!" they said. But, they found the silver cup in Benjamin's pouch. The soldiers brought them back to Joseph.

Judah said, "God is punishing us for our guilt. We will be your slaves." Joseph said, "Only Benjamin will be my slave, for he stole the goblet." Judah said, "Please sir, my father is old. He had twelve sons, but one is dead. Now, if Benjamin doesn't return, our father will die of sorrow. Please let me stay in Benjamin's place."

Joseph could not control himself, and sent all of his servants out of the room. Then Joseph broke down and cried. Joseph said to his brothers, "Come near to me. I am Joseph your brother, whom you sold into Egypt. Don't be distressed because you sold me here; for God sent me before you to preserve life. You meant to do evil, but God used it to do good. We have had famine for two years now, but another five years of famine will follow. Hurry and get our father, and your wives and children, and bring them here. They will have food to eat and they can live" (Genesis 45:4-9).

Joseph's brothers hurried back to tell their father that Joseph was alive! They were so happy. Israel was happy. Do you see how God brought good out of evil? How do you think Joseph's brothers felt about how mean they were to Joseph when they were young? Try to be good and nice to people all the time. It makes God happy when we are kind.

ACT OF LOVE

O my God,
I love you above all things with my whole heart and soul,
because You are all good and worthy of all my love.
I love my neighbor as myself for the love of You.
I forgive all who have injured me,
and ask pardon for all whom I have injured.

ACT OF LOVE

O my God,

I love you above all things

with my whole heart and soul,

because You are all good

and worthy of all my love.

I love my neighbor as myself

for the love of You.

I forgive all who have injured me,

and ask pardon for all whom

I have injured.

Joseph Saves His Family

Craft — Joseph Saves His Family

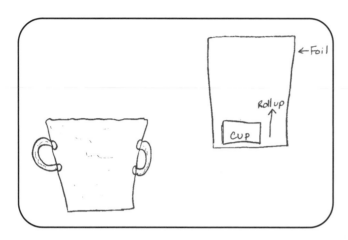

This special craft will make a silver cup like the one Joseph hid in Benjamin's sack.

Materials:
5-ounce paper cups, cotton swabs, aluminum foil, hole puncher, and scissors.

Preparation:
1. Cut strips of aluminum foil in 5" widths.

Assembling:
1. Place the cup at one end of the aluminum foil and roll it up, tucking in extra foil. This creates the silver cup.

2. Punch two holes on each side of the cup (hint: place the hole puncher in as far as it will go (punch) then bring out the puncher halfway from the original hole to the lip of the cup (punch)).

3. Wrap aluminum foil around two cotton swabs.

4. Insert the wrapped cotton swabs into the two holes and bend the tip inside the cup. This make the cup's handles, giving the cup a "goblet" look.

Other ideas:
1. Decorate little brown lunch bags to create sacks and simulate how the cup was hidden in the sack.

2. Use bag ties if cotton swabs aren't available.

Blessings

Genesis 48-50

Memory Verse:
**"God Almighty will bless you
with blessings of heaven above."
(Genesis 49:25)**

Jacob was so happy to learn that his son Joseph was alive. He packed his things and started out for Egypt. On the way, God spoke to Israel in the night and said, "Jacob, Jacob." And Israel said, "Here I am." God said, "I am God, the God of your father. Don't be afraid to go down to Egypt, for I will be with you and I will make of you a great nation, and then I will bring you back again."

Israel's sons, their wives, and children numbered sixty-six people in all. Isn't that a big family? They all traveled together to Egypt to meet Joseph, because they were all very hungry and Joseph had food stored away for them.

Joseph rode in a chariot to meet his father and his brothers. Joseph fell on his father's neck and cried. He was so happy to see his father after so many years! Joseph presented his father to Pharaoh and asked for land on which to settle his brothers and their families. Since they were shepherds, they settled in the land of Goshen, which had good grass for the sheep.

When Israel was an old man, he called his sons and grandsons together, to say good-bye to them before he died. Israel blessed all of his sons, and then he breathed his last, and was gathered to his people.

When their father died, Joseph's brothers thought that Joseph would pay them back for selling him into slavery. But Joseph forgave his brothers. "You meant evil against me; but God meant it for good to keep many people alive" (Genesis 50:20). Joseph knew that he could not be in the place of God. Only God has the right to punish and to bless. So, Joseph took care of his brothers and their families. Joseph lived to be very old, and saw his grandchildren and great-grandchildren.

Didn't Joseph live an exciting life? Joseph saved his family from death due to starvation. Jesus came to save us from eternal death, due to our sins. The story of Joseph gets our minds and our hearts ready for the story of Jesus. Jesus saves sinners for all time!

Blessings

Craft — Blessings

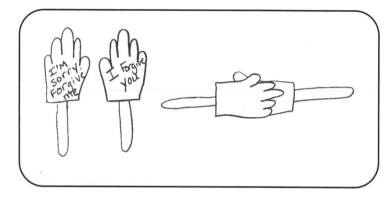

This craft will make two hand puppets that can shake hands and be used to teach children forgiveness.

Materials:
Craft sticks, construction paper, crayons or markers, glue, pencil, and scissors.

Preparation:
1. Trace and cut a pattern of an adult size left hand print and a right hand print (fingers closed with thumb up).

Assembling:
1. Fold one piece of construction paper in half and cut.
2. Trace and cut a left hand print. Write "I'm sorry, Please forgive me" in the palm of the left hand using crayons or markers.
3. Trace and cut a right hand print. Write "I Forgive You" in the palm of the right hand using crayons or markers.
4. Glue the hands to the craft stick so that the writings will be showing. The back of both thumbs should line up as well as the finger tips.
5. Have the children practice shaking hands with each other, saying, "I'm sorry, please forgive me," and the other responding, "I forgive you."

Other ideas:
1. Decorate the fingers and hands of the craft by drawing rings, fingernails a watch or bracelet.
2. For older children, allow them to trace and cut their own hand prints.